CONTENTS

INTRODUCTION

Tennis is a great action sport which can be played and enjoyed by all ages from 4 to 80 and beyond! If you are a complete beginner, a regular player or haven't played for some time, this book can help you – from finding your local courts to improving your serve or forehand. It explains the rules, equipment and court as well as guiding you through the key techniques, tactics and the mental side of the game. There is also information on Ariel Mini Tennis, the modified version of the game to help players under 10 years of age, and Raw Tennis, the new programme to help 10–18s improve their skills and enjoyment of the sport.

Do More Than Just Watch – Play Tennis

THE COURT

Tennis is played on a marked out area known as a court. The game was born on grass although it is now played on a variety of different surfaces. These include clay courts found mainly in Europe and South America, cement courts, artificial grass and indoor courts using a form of carpet or cushioned acrylic. Different surfaces see the ball bounce and move in different ways. For example cement courts and grass (when cut short and the ground is hard) are fast surfaces. Other surfaces such as clay slow the ball down and allow it to be returned more easily.

ADJUSTING THE NET

The net should be 3 ft (0.91m) high at the centre service line (see diagram). It is held in place by net posts and adjusted using the net post winder and the centre band adjustment.

Tennis is one of the few sports played on a variety of different surfaces.

Rafael Nadal prepares for a forehand from behind the baseline.

The tennis court is the same length for doubles (two players per side) and singles (one player per side). For doubles, it is 9 ft (2.74m) wider. The area between the sidelines of the singles and doubles court is known as the tramlines.

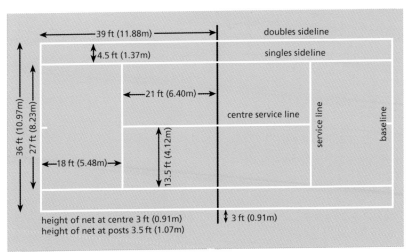

39 ft (11.88m)

doubles sideline

4.5 ft (1.37m)

singles sideline

36 ft (10.97m)

27 ft (8.23m)

21 ft (6.40m)

centre service line

service line

baseline

13.5 ft (4.12m)

18 ft (5.48m)

height of net at centre 3 ft (0.91m)
height of net at posts 3.5 ft (1.07m)

3 ft (0.91m)

EQUIPMENT

Equipment in tennis has progressed significantly over recent years. From rackets with wooden frames and all-white cotton clothing, to rackets designed with space-age materials and high performance coloured kit – the changes could not be more dramatic.

RACKETS

Choosing the correct racket for you is crucial. The right choice will result in hours of fun and satisfaction. The wrong decision could result in frustration or even injury.

There is a huge range of models available. Rackets vary in price, length, head size, weight and their stiffness or flex. They are made out of different materials, from aluminium to graphite, and are often reinforced with titanium and other space-age materials. How much you should pay depends on how often you play. If you play regularly, it is worth considering a more expensive technical racket.

RACKETS FOR ADULTS

A racket's weight is measured as:

- under 10 oz (285g) – light
- 10–11.5 oz (285–325g) – medium
- over 11.5 oz (325g) – heavy.

For adults new to the game a light, medium-to-stiff racket is generally recommended. It will be less tiring on the arm and will aid comfort and ease of swing.

Length and Width

A standard length adult racket is 27 in (68.5cm), but 'long body' rackets go up to 29 in (73.6cm) in length. These help give extra power. They also allow players who are shorter in height or slower on their feet to reach balls slightly further away. The frame profile is the width of the racket frame when looked at side on. Beginners should consider wide-body frames (between 24 and 30mm) as these are stiffer and more powerful.

Racket Head Size

Racket heads range in area from 90 sq in (600sq cm) to an oversize 120 sq in (770sq cm). Smaller-headed rackets provide more ball feel and are chosen usually by more advanced players. A larger-headed racket has a bigger 'sweet-spot' – the area of the racket's strings which produce the best mixture of feel and power. This makes them ideal for newer players.

Grip Sizing

The correct grip size (handle size) will depend on how big your hand is. If you find your racket is slipping in your hand, try using an over-grip designed to soak up sweat. An over-grip tends to increase the grip by half a size.

Get advice on your grip size and which racket is most suitable for you from a tennis coach or at a good sports shop.

Your racket should be comfortable and east to wield.

RACKETS FOR JUNIORS

It is important the racket is the right size for a young player so that they get the best from their tennis and don't risk hurting themselves. Rackets increase in size as the junior player grows. They start at 19 in (48.25cm) long for toddlers and go up to 26.25 in (66.7cm) – only 0.75 in (1.9cm) shorter than an adult standard length racket.

A cheaper aluminium racket is suitable for complete beginners. But as players improve and play more regularly, they may want to consider a composite racket made of aluminium and graphite.

TENNIS BALLS

Regular tennis balls come in two types: pressure-less and pressurised. Pressure-less balls are cheaper and longer lasting. Pressurised balls are inflated during manufacture. They are more expensive and wear out quicker but bounce at a more manageable height and speed. They are used in most official competitions.

Mini Tennis balls

For younger juniors, Mini Tennis balls (see page 54–55) are recommended. They come in a variety of types which bounce at different speeds and heights. They help children of different ages and abilities to play correct shots without straining their joints.

 Juniors learning about the different makes of tennis balls.

 Mini Tennis is played with shorter rackets and a lower-bouncing ball.

SHOES

Do not wear running shoes or
fashion trainers to play tennis.
Unlike running, tennis involves
sideways movement, pushing off
the balls of your feet. Wearing the
wrong shoes can hinder your
performance and even cause injury.
Proper tennis shoes are built with
features in their soles and uppers to
provide support and stability for
sideways movement. Tennis is also
a high impact activity so make sure
your shoes have good cushioning
inside which help absorb shock.

CLOTHING

Tennis is a fast and athletic game so
clothing needs to be comfortable and
not restrict your body movement.

Fabrics used in modern-day tennis
wear are designed to keep the
player cool and dry plus protect
against UV light.

Shorts and shirts (short sleeved
and sleeveless polo's and T-shirts)
are the norm for men and skirts,
shorts, tops and dresses for
women. Tracksuits are worn by
both sexes for warmth before
and after play.

Tennis clothes are designed
for performance and fashion.

RULES

It is rare to have an umpire in tennis. Even in official tournaments, umpires are usually only available on finals day. Each player normally calls the balls on their side of the net, and the players umpire the match themselves – it is important to know the rules!

SINGLES

The game is started by one player serving the ball. The question of who serves first and who has the choice of ends is decided by a toss. The winner of the toss can make one of four decisions:

- decide to serve – in which case the opponent has choice of ends

- decide to receive – in which case the opponent has choice of ends

- choose ends – in which case the opponent may choose to serve or receive

- ask the opponent to choose.

A service stroke is completed when the server attempts to strike the ball. A service is in play if it passes over the net without bouncing and falls within the service court diagonally opposite the server.

The server has a second attempt to do this in each point if his first service is a fault. After each point has been scored, the server changes to the other side of the centre mark for the next service point, and so on.

Completing a game

After completing the first game, the player who was the receiver becomes the server in the next game. The players then serve in alternate games until the end of the match. The only exception to this is if the players are in a tie-break (see page 20).

POSITIONS FOR SERVICE

The first point of the game is started with the server standing behind the baseline. They must also stand between two imaginary lines drawn down from the centre marking and the right-hand singles line. The receiver can take up any position he chooses on his side of the net.

SERVICE

In delivering the service the server should:

- place the ball into the air by hand

- keep both feet to the correct side of the centre mark and not touch the baseline or court with their feet

- strike the ball with his racket before it reaches the ground. If the server places the ball into the air but doesn't attempt a stroke then it is a let (see below). If he attempts a stroke but misses the ball completely then it is a fault

- not serve until the receiver is ready.

If the receiver is not ready when the serve is made a let is called. This means that the service does not count and is taken again. If, however, the receiver attempts to play the ball he cannot then claim a let for not being ready.

The winner of the toss can ask their opponent to choose ends or to serve or receive first.

The server must not touch the line or court before hitting the ball.

Serving out of turn

If a player serves out of turn, the player who should have served must serve as soon as the mistake is discovered. All points scored up to this discovery will stand but a single fault served before the discovery is made does not count. If the entire game is completed before the discovery is made, the order of the service remains as altered.

Faults

If the first service is a fault, the server is allowed one more service. This must be taken from the correct side of the court. If the second service is a fault, a 'double fault' is called and the server loses the point.

A service ball striking the net, strap or band and bouncing directly into the correct service court is a let. This service is played again. If the ball hits any other fixture other than the net when served, then it is a fault.

If a serve strikes a loose ball in the service box, you can play on as long as you hit the correct ball!

Foot faults

A foot fault is counted just like any other fault. It occurs if at any time during the service motion the server:

- touches the court or baseline with either foot
- is on the wrong side of the baseline centre mark
- is beyond the imaginary extension of the sideline.

Serving without foot faulting – with varying success!

IN AND OUT OF PLAY

A ball is in play from the moment it is delivered in service (unless a fault or let is given). It remains in play until the point is decided.

Ball touching permanent fixture

If the ball in play touches a permanent fixture (other than the net, posts, centre strap or net band) before it bounces, the striker of the ball loses the point. If it strikes the permanent fixture after it has bounced then his opponent loses the point.

Ball in court

The ball does not have to land entirely inside the court to stay in play. Rule 12 of the rules of tennis states that 'if a ball touches the line, it is regarded as touching the court bounded by that line'. This means that if any part of the ball bounces on the boundary lines of a tennis court, then the ball is in play.

> **If any part of the ball touches the line, it is in play.**

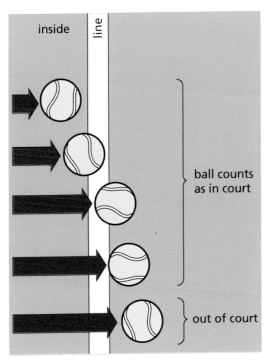

◀ As long as the ball is touching part of the sideline or baseline as it bounces, it is in court. Only the bottom ball in the diagram is out of court.

inside   line

ball counts as in court

out of court

RETURNING SERVICE

A player is allowed to stand anywhere on their side of the court and behind the baseline to receive a service. The player receiving the serve makes a good return if:

- they return the ball directly into their opponent's court before it bounces twice on their own side of the net

- the ball touches the net, post, centre strap or net band, but passes over the net and falls within the opponent's court

- the ball is returned outside of the net posts above or below the level of the top of the net and drops within the proper court

- a player succeeds in returning the ball which has struck another ball lying on the court.

If the ball bounces back over the net, the player on whose side it bounced can reach over the net to play the ball. It is only a good return if neither he nor his racket touch the net, post or ground on his opponent's side.

Losing the point

The player receiving the service does not make a good return and loses the point if:

- they hit the ball on the volley before it has bounced on their side of the net

- they deliberately carry or catch the ball on their racket or deliberately touch it with their racket more than once

- they throw their racket which hits the ball

- the ball touches the player or anything he wears or carries (except the racket) whilst the ball is in play

- they strike the ball before it has crossed the net.

Maria Sharapova makes a return.

CHANGE OF ENDS

The players change the end that they play from after the finish of the first and third game of a set. They then continue to change ends every second game until the set finishes.

Odd and even

If at the end of the set, the number of games played in that set was even, the players return to the same ends for the first game of the next set after their set break.

When the number of games played at the end of a set was uneven, the players change ends after the set break. This means that the first game of the next set occurs with the players changing ends. The players change ends again after the first, third, fifth games and so on until this new set is completed.

Changing ends means that both payers can take on refreshments and have to deal with the same conditions through the course of the match.

SCORING

Game

The points in a game that a player has are called as follows:

- Love – no points
- Fifteen – 1 point
- Thirty – 2 points
- Forty – 3 points
- Game – 4 points or winning from advantage in deuce (see below). The game is won and the next game played.

The server's score is always given first. So, for example, if the server wins the first point, the score will be Fifteen–Love. If the server loses the first point of the match, then the score would be Love–Fifteen. If the server wins the first two points of the game, the score is Thirty–Love. If the receiver wins the next three points the score will be Thirty–Forty. Whenever the game is tied with the players on the same number of points, the score is given as that number of points to all, e.g. Fifteen–All or Thirty–All.

Deuce

If the players score three points each, instead of the score being Forty–All, it is said to be Deuce. In this case one or the other player must win two points in a row to win the game. If the server wins the first point after deuce, the score is Advantage server. If the receiver wins the point the score is Advantage receiver.

If the player with the advantage loses the next point, the score returns to Deuce. The game continues for as many points as are necessary until one of the players leads by two points to win the game.

When a serving player wins the game without his or her opponent scoring a point, they are said to have, 'won the game to love'.

Jayant Mistry in action in the final of the Men's Wheelchair Doubles tournament at Wimbledon.

Set

The first player (or pair in a doubles match) to win six games wins the set. In an 'advantage set', if the score reaches five–all one player or pair must go two games ahead to win. In a 'tie–break' set, if the score reaches six–all a tie-break is played (see page 20).

Match

The maximum number of sets in a match is five for men and three for women. Local tournament rules usually state the number and type of sets to be played in a match. Normally, matches are decided on the best of three tie-break sets. Some tournaments – such as Wimbledon – play tie-break sets with the final set an advantage set.

LONG SET!

At the 2003 Australian Open, Andy Roddick finally beat Younes Aynaoui in the fifth and final set of their quarter final match. The fifth set lasted for 40 games before ending 21–19 in Roddick's favour.

Always keep note of the score when you're playing a match.

Andy Roddick in action.

DOUBLES

Doubles matches have two players per side and can be mixed or single sex. Service and choice of ends are decided in the same way as for singles (see p10).

Order of service

The pair serving first must decide which partner will serve in the opening game. The opposing pair decides who will serve in the second game.

Each doubles pair serves a game alternately. For example, the pair containing players **A** and **B** (below) win the toss and decide that player **A** will serve first. The opposing team decide that player **C** will serve their first game. After player **A** has served their game and player **C** theirs, player **B** will serve followed by player **D**. This order of service will continue until the set is ended.

see p10

SERVING AND RECEIVING CHOICE

There is no rule requiring the player who receives first in the first game to serve in the second game. In the diagram, player **C** may choose to receive serve in the first game but either they or player **D** can serve in the next. Whichever player starts serving, they must do so from the right side.

The server, **A**, stands behind the baseline between an imaginary continuation of the centre mark and the doubles sideline (the outer tramline). He serves across the court to player **C**, who is the receiver.

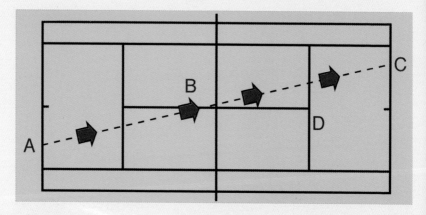

Ball touching server's partner

The service is a fault if:

- the ball touches the server's partner

- the ball touches anything that the server's partner wears or carries.

Ball touching receiver's partner

A good service sees the server win the point if:

- the ball touches the receiver's partner

- the ball touches the receiver's partner's clothing or anything he carries.

Serving out of turn

If a player serves out of turn the partner who ought to have served must serve as soon as the mistake is discovered. Any points scored and any fault served before the discovery stands. If a game is completed before the mistake is discovered, the order of serving will remain as altered.

Order of receiving service

Partners must decide who receives in the right court and who in the left. Once the right court player (**C** in the diagram on page 18) has stood to receive service, neither he nor his partner can change their positions for receiving service until the start of a new set.

Error in receiving order

If a player receives in the wrong court, they continue in that court until the end of the game. They revert to their correct court in the next game of the set in which the pair receives.

Venus and Serena Williams in doubles action at Wimbledon.

THE TIE-BREAK

In a tie-break set, the tie-break operates at six games all.

Singles

To win a tie-break, a player has to win seven points and lead by two points. If the score reaches six points all, the game continues until one player gets two points ahead.

The player whose turn it is to serve serves the first point. His opponent serves the second and third points, and from that point on, each player serves alternately for two points in a row until there is a winner. The person who served the first point in the tie-break, receives in the first game of the next set.

In a tie-break:

- numerical scoring (1, 2, 3) is used rather than regular game scoring (15, 30, 40)

- each service should be delivered alternately from the right and left courts, beginning from the right court

- players change ends after every six points and at the end of the tie-break.

ORGANISERS' DECISIONS

The Organising Committee must decide and announce before the start of any tournament, match or competition whether matches will be best of three or five sets, whether tie-break or advantage set (or a combination) will be played, and whether a 'deciding match tie-break' will be used in place of a final set.

Marat Safin consults with the umpire during a game.

Doubles

The tie-break in doubles works in the same way to singles. The player whose turn it is to serve will serve for the first point. After that, each player serves for two points in rotation and in the same order as previously in that set. Serving goes on until the winners of the tie-break and, therefore, the game and set have been decided.

Deciding match tie-break

Tennis's world governing body, the International Tennis Federation (ITF), has agreed that a tie-break can be used in place of a final set to decide a match. The 'deciding match tie-break' can be the first to seven by two clear point (as described above), or the first to ten by two clear points, which is commonly referred to as a 'champion's tie-break'.

▼ Tim Henman, a player with a strong history of winning tie-breaks at Wimbledon.

TACTICS

Many people start to play tennis because they are interested in the competitive and strategic side of the game. They are concerned with tactics – how to play the game and how to win points.

TECHNIQUE AND TACTICS

There is much important crossover between technique and tactics. The better your tactics, the more you can make your shots count whilst the better your shots, the more tactical options you have available. For example, if you don't have the correct technique to hit topspin shots (see page 42), the tactic of playing sharp-angled shots to move your opponent is limited.

GAME SITUATIONS

Tactics are best examined and explained by looking at the most common situations players find themselves in on the court. These are known as, 'game situations'.

The basic game situations are:

- when a player is serving
- when a player is receiving
- when both players are at the back of the court (around the baseline)
- when a player is approaching or at the net
- when the opponent is approaching or at the net.

Guillermo Coria returns a sharp-angled shot.

> **How to plan to win points is known as your tactics. How to hit the ball is known as technique.**

BASIC TACTICS

Whatever the game situation, players will also need to be able to implement the basic tactics. The basic tactics remain the same whatever the game situation.

Put and keep the ball in play

It is not necessary to hit 'winners' to win matches. Most matches are lost by a player making too many mistakes. If a player always returns the ball into play he is likely to force his opponent into errors.

Errors are split into two types:

- forced errors – when the error came as a result of being put under pressure by a good shot from the opponent

- unforced errors – when the error was made without the opponent making the shot difficult.

Good technique is best learned when young from a qualified coach. An LTA-licensed coach is qualified, CRB checked and up to date.

To get the ball in, it simply needs to travel:

- over the net, and
- into the court.

The best way to develop consistency in keeping shots in play from the baseline is by hitting forehand and backhand shots with a curving flight path shaped like a humped-back bridge.

The good player develops a balance between consistency and aggression. They combine softer shots with harder ones. As players improve, this balance becomes even more important. Making the choice of which shot to use when is known as 'shot selection'. Good shot selection plays an important role in consistency.

Hitting cross court

As a general rule, it is safer and better to hit the ball diagonally 'cross court' when rallying from the baseline. This is for a number of reasons:

- the ball travelling cross court crosses the net at the middle, where it is 6 in (15cm) lower
- the distance is diagonal and therefore longer; it is easier to move the opponent by using an angle

- it is the natural direction of the racket swing
- it is easier to return the ball where it came from than it is to change direction (each rally begins cross court with a serve)
- court positioning for the next ball is easier.

Good court positioning

The better your position on the court in relation to the play, the easier it is to execute your shot. The basic positions for singles are shown here and for doubles on pages 28–29.

Many players understand that they need to move quickly to get to the ball to retrieve an opponent's shot. Yet, they often fail to use the same quick movements to get into a good, ready position straight after they have hit their own shot.

For beginners, the best place to recover to is the middle of the court. As a player progresses, they find that the best place to recover to is in fact the middle of all possible shots that their opponent can hit. This is like a football goalkeeper, positioning himself not in the middle of his goal but at the right angle to cover the gaps if an attack is coming from the side.

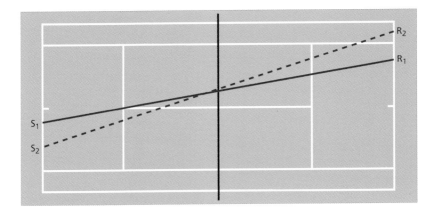

Basic positions – service and return

With the server (**S1**) close to the centre mark, the receiver (**R1**) positions himself to cover both sides of the service area. If the server (**S2**) goes wider to get more angle in their serve, the receiver (**R2**) adjusts his position.

Roger Federer moves round to attack with a forehand return from a second serve.

Make your opponent run

By making your opponent move, spaces are created that can be aimed at, putting more pressure on the opponent's movement and technique. Hitting to the space once it has been created is a well-known tactic in tennis.

At a higher level, players know this and may do the opposite. They hit the ball not into the space but away from it. The idea is that their opponent will run towards the space expecting the ball to be sent there. The result is that the opponent runs away from the ball. This is called a wrong-footing shot.

It's easier to move an opponent by hitting cross court than down the line as you have more of an angle to work with.

Tim Henman – one of the world's best volleyers – plays a wrong footing shot.

Exploit a weakness

All players have weaknesses. Sometimes, the weakness is obvious like a poor backhand. Other times, the weakness is more subtle such as a player only able to hit a shot in one direction. Seek out an opponent's weakness and if you find it, take advantage of it and try to play the ball to that weakness. This increases the chances of them making an error.

An opponent's weakness can often influence your court position. For example, an opponent may not be able to lob. This may influence the player to come in closer to the net knowing that they will not be lobbed.

Use your strengths

Like all players you will have some shots that are stronger than others. Many beginners, for example, find that their forehand is stronger than their backhand.

The more often you can use your strengths, the more success you are likely to have. Try, when you can, to use your strengths against your opponent's weaknesses. An example of this would be a strong forehand hit to your opponent's weak backhand.

Players often take a court position to use their strengths more effectively. This may mean they leave a bigger gap on their stronger side when they are on the baseline. They then run around to hit their favourite shot. An example of this is when players run around to hit a forehand where a backhand would normally be hit. This type of shot is called an 'inside out' or 'off' forehand.

Justine Henin-Hardenne plays an inside-out forehand from the backhand corner of the court.

DOUBLES

Many players feel more relaxed in doubles than in singles, and enjoy the shared responsibility. However, doubles still requires good tactics and strategy and, as part of a team, you must be aware of the strengths and weaknesses of both your partner and your opposition.

In doubles, players will change their positions to develop possible winning positions (see diagrams on page 29). Basic tactics are:

- play as a team
- attack the weaker opponent
- retain good positions on court
- use the angles of play
- focus on getting your first serve in.

Play as a team

This means that both players should work together. This can only be done through communicating frequently, encouraging each other and agreeing which tactics to follow.

Play to the weaker opponent

One player in a partnership will be weaker than the other. By playing more returns to that player, it is easier to win the point. Note that the weaker partner may be different at different times. For example, a very strong server may be weaker at volleying.

Return serve low and to server

It is very important for the receiver to make the server play the return of serve. If the return is kept low it is more difficult for a player coming to the net after their serve to hit a volley. A higher return allows the server or their partner to volley the ball and win the point.

Interceptions

Whilst players cover their own half of the net, it is common to see the net player cross to their partner's side to 'intercept' the ball on the volley, especially a high ball that is easier for the net player to finish off.

Get to the net

In doubles, the team which can get to the net first is more likely to win the point. When at the net, the pair should play together alongside each other. They should move as if joined together so that if one moves left so does the other to cover the gap down the middle.

GET THE FIRST SERVE IN

In doubles, it is vital to win the serve especially to the weaker opponent. Some pace can be reduced to give more accuracy and give the server a greater chance of getting to the net if serve and volleying.

Use the angles of play

The doubles court is wider than the singles court. Playing angled shots opens up the court and makes it more difficult for a team to cover the possible returns.

The tactical plan should be to use the angles of the court when in control of the point by playing the ball wide into the tramlines. Try to stop opponents using the same tactic when they are in control of the point by hitting down the centre, reducing their ability to hit an angle. If the ball is hit down the centre it may also lead to indecision on the part of the opponents.

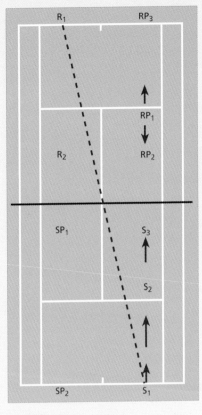

Doubles positions – rallying

In this diagram the server has moved from the baseline (**S1**) through the midcourt (**S2**) to the net (**S3**) to form an attacking position with their partner (**SP1**).

Doubles positions – serve and return

The server (**S1**) stands a little wider than for singles. Their partner (**SP1**) stands close to the net ready to intercept and volley a loose return. The receiver's partner (**RP1**) stands just outside the service area.

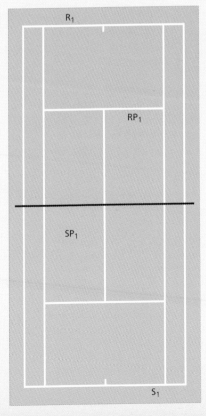

THE MENTAL GAME

The mind is a powerful tool in sport. Thoughts and feelings affect all other areas of the game. In tennis, most of the time on court is spent not hitting the ball, but in between points – so there is plenty of time to think.

REASONS FOR PLAYING

Do you play tennis to meet people and socialise or because your friends play? Do you play to get physical exercise, to win competitions, purely for enjoyment or, maybe, a combination of these things? Whatever your reasons, try to remember them and keep your own basic motives for playing, but try to gradually introduce other areas to add to your pleasure of the game.

Don't let a bad shot rattle you. Put it out of your mind and focus on the next shot and the next point.

USE YOUR MIND

The better players are not always those with the best technique or physique. Vast numbers of matches are won by players up against a tough opponent who may appear faster, fitter or have better skills than them. Many of these matches are won because players are able to use their mind to keep the correct mental attitude and to plot a way of winning even though the advantages are in their opponent's favour. What do you need to be successful in developing the right mental attitude? Here are some pointers.

AWARENESS

Your method of play

Are you steady and consistent, or aggressive and happy to take risks? Whatever your method and style of play try to recognise and be aware of your strengths and weaknesses. Once you know them, you can plan the way you play around them.

Opponent's method of play

Can you 'read' your opponent's method and style of play? Have you noticed if they cover up a weakness, such as running around to their forehand to avoid their backhand? Maybe, the way they tend to move leaves gaps on their side of the court which you can attack? As discussed earlier, using your strengths to attack an opponent's weakness is effective.

Although tennis is an all-action sport, tactics and matchplay are a lot like chess, with both players trying to outwit each other. The difference is that you have just moments to make crucial decisions. There's a limited time between shots in tennis so you need to be able to make decisions rapidly.

Assessing your performance

In competition, it is very easy to think, 'I won so I played well' or, 'I lost so I played badly'. It is vital to understand the difference between the result and your performance. Sometimes, you may lose a match but play extremely well. On other occasions, you may play poorly and make many wrong tactical decisions yet still win. Be honest about how you played.

 Richard Gasquet unleashes an attacking forehand.

TAKING ON THE CHALLENGE

Tennis offers a different challenge each time you head onto the court and face an opponent. Look forward to each challenge as a positive test of your abilities. Possessing the following will help you.

Concentration

When playing tennis – from keeping score to watching for spin on the ball – you need a high level of concentration or 'focus'. Try to focus on one thing. If you flit from one thing to another, you will find it hard to concentrate well. For example, a positive aid to concentrating on the flight of the ball is to say quietly 'bounce' exactly as the ball bounces and 'hit' as you make contact.

Confidence

Confidence comes from self-belief in your ability to reach a level of performance that you have set as your current goal. Set realistic goals you can achieve and work towards them. Achieving these goals will help you develop a high level of confidence.

Competitiveness

Competitiveness comes from the love of a challenge. A true competitor is one who enjoys the battle and 'hangs in' all the way, whether they are in front or behind. In every tennis match there is always one winner and one loser, but there should always be two competitors. If you have tried to give of your best all the way, there can be no disgrace in defeat. The real competition is the one you have with yourself and your game.

 Lleyton Hewitt is well known for his fighting qualities on court.

SPORTSMANSHIP

Tennis provides a wonderful opportunity to meet and compete with others. However, as well as written rules and regulations, there are also unwritten codes of behaviour.

When playing and competing make sure you behave as you would wish others to behave towards you. In other words:

- try to appreciate not only your own good play but also your opponent's

- be fair and honest about all decisions and calls

- never abuse officials, opponents or spectators

- don't let your strong desire to win get in the way of acting in a sporting way.

Good tennis players at all levels of ability learn from defeats but also learn to put defeats behind them and to be courteous and sociable after a game. For the vast majority of tennis players, the sport is played for fun. Never forget that.

Never give up in a match. Many matches are turned around from seemingly impossible positions.

Paradorn Srichaphan is known among his fellow players for being a good sportsman.

TECHNIQUES

The way a player hits the ball is known as their technique. There are many techniques and not all players use the same ones. There are, however, some common points which ensure good basic technique.

GRIPS

How you hold the racket is your grip and is absolutely vital to your tennis success. Your grip needs to be strong but flexible and, most important, comfortable. The following are the most effective grips for specific shots.

▲ Eastern forehand grip.

Eastern forehand

This is known as the 'shake hands' grip because the palm is placed behind the handle and the thumb is wrapped round the grip as though 'shaking hands' with the racket. The index finger is slightly spread apart from the middle finger.

This grip is good for the forehand drive (see page 37) allowing you to hit balls of different heights with good strength. In addition, it can be used for the forehand volley, the lob and, for beginners, their first steps in serving.

▲ Semi-Western forehand grip.

Semi-Western forehand

This grip is used mainly for the forehand drive. The palm lies more underneath the handle. This grip makes it easier to hit balls that are above waist height, and leads to aggressive forehand shots.

Eastern backhand

This is an effective grip used for the backhand drive (see pages 39 and 41). Often players wrap their thumb around the back. This is a very sensitive and strong grip.

Two-handed backhand

The two-handed backhand provides greater strength and control for beginners than a one-handed backhand. Both hands should be close together and touching each other on the handle without overlapping.

 Eastern backhand grip.

 Chopper grip.

Junior beginners may choose to hold the racket using an Eastern forehand grip for both hands. More able players should alter this as soon as they can for more power and control. The hand nearest the end of the racket should use a continental, or if physically stronger, an Eastern backhand, grip. The added hand should employ an Eastern forehand grip.

Chopper or continental

The chopper grip is used mainly for the service and for advanced stages of the volley. It is halfway between the Eastern forehand and backhand, and involves placing the palm of the hand on top of the racket for the service, similar to how you might hold a hammer. It provides greater racket head speed, flexibility and variation for the serve than the straightforward forehand grip.

Two-handed backhand with right hand chopper and left hand Eastern grip.

BASIC STROKES FOR BEGINNERS

Many different factors go into how well a player hits the ball. Some of these happen before the ball has even bounced. The essentials of good technique are described below in the order that they happen on the court.

GROUNDSTROKES

Forehands and backhands played from the baseline are known as 'groundstrokes' (and sometimes 'drives'). There are many similarities between both the forehand and backhand groundstrokes. The following key points are relevant to both shots.

Whether playing groundstrokes or volleying, you must begin from what is called the ready position (see page 24). This enables you to start quickly, and be ready to play either a forehand or a backhand shot.

Reading the ball

Quick forwards, backwards and sideways movement is absolutely vital in tennis. But getting quickly into the right position and staying balanced is not just to do with footwork. The better that a player can 'read' the ball, the quicker they will be able to move into the correct position.

To do this, players need to be aware of the different flight paths of the ball in tennis and to be able to

recognise them as the ball travels towards them. Factors which affect the flight path of the ball include:

- the speed with which the ball is hit

- the position on the court from where it was hit

- the spin used by their opponent

- the court surface

- the height of the shot.

Players have to read and predict the depth of an incoming shot. For example, a softly hit shot with no spin will land shorter in the court. They must also be able to calculate the likely bounce. For example, a high loopy flight path is likely to result in a high bounce whilst a hard and low flight path is likely to result in a fast, low bounce.

Beginners often run to where the ball is going to bounce, instead of to where the ball will be at the right height to hit after the bounce. This skill tends to improve with experience. Top players seem to know where the ball is going and appear to be waiting for it to arrive. This seemingly effortless skill is the result of great experience and many hours of hard work and practice.

> **Always watch the ball and its flight path, trying to read and anticipate where it will end up.**

Justine Henin-Hardenne moves into position and prepares to hit a forehand.

She takes her racket back and maintains good balance.

She swings her racket from beneath the height of the ball, to contact the ball to the side and in front.

She follows through high and across her body.

MOVEMENT AND BALANCE

Whether you have good technique or merely want to get on with playing the game casually, coordinating the racket swing to the ball is often the biggest challenge. It requires good footwork and balance. In a rally the opponent will move the ball around the court, so you need to be able to react to and read the incoming ball. The aim is to move into a position for a good contact point (see below) with the ball whilst keeping your balance throughout the shot.

Tennis is a fast-moving game so it is not always possible to be in perfect position. But you can move your feet to get into an approximate position quickly and then make smaller adjustments to your footwork so that you can get balanced and in the best possible position. You need to make fast initial movement before slowing down to gain balance just before the ball arrives.

To judge how good your footwork and balance is, be aware of what happens after you hit the ball. If you were balanced after the hit it is likely you were in control of the ball. If you are making recovery steps to get back on balance immediately after the hit, then it is likely that the ball was in control of you!

Stance

Stance refers to the position of the body and the feet as the ball comes towards you. For beginners, being sideways to the ball on both forehand and backhand strokes is advisable. This allows for a basic swing path to be developed more easily. As a player gets better, the stance of the feet may vary, but the shoulders will always turn sideways to the ball as part of their shot preparation.

Contact point

Where you hit the ball in relation to your body is known as the 'contact point'. The position of the contact in relation to the body is pinpointed by three dimensions:

- the height of the contact in relation to your body
- the distance of the contact from your body to the side
- the distance of the contact from your body in front/behind.

Generally speaking, the contact point should be comfortably in front of your body and comfortably to the side.

DOUBLE–HANDED BACKHAND

Gael Monfils gets into position with a sideways-on stance.

As the racket head swings forward it drops below the height of the ball.

He follows through from low to high.

Kim Clijsters demonstrates the contact point. The height may vary depending on the incoming ball and tactical intention.

Height of contact point

The height of the contact point can vary depending on:

- the grip used
- the height of the incoming ball
- the surface played on
- the tactical intention
- the standard of player.

To give some examples, a first serve will not bounce as high as a groundstroke whilst a ball bounces higher on hard courts than on artificial grass courts. Attacking shots are better taken above net height whilst a player with a semi-Western grip will be able to contact a higher ball more comfortably than a player with an Eastern grip.

The easiest time for beginners to contact the ball is after the ball has reached the top of its bounce (the highest point) and is just beginning to fall towards what would be its second bounce.

Action

The 'action' is as vital as the contact point. The racket travels through the ball. Beginners often 'push' the ball into play because they don't want to let the racket get too far away from the imagined contact point in case they miss it when it arrives. However, for greater power, the racket should be swung at the ball, building up speed to the contact point and following through after higher than the contact.
The path that the racket travels is known as the 'swing path'. Starting from the ready position (see page 24), the swing paths are broken down into the 'take back' and the 'follow through'. In simple terms:

- the take back involves taking the racket back early whilst turning the shoulders so that the ball can be played from the side
- the follow through for groundstrokes is from low through the contact point to high with the racket travelling above the ball after the contact.

Rafael Nadal unleashes a forehand.

SINGLE-HANDED BACKHAND

Roger Federer begins to take his racket back as he reads the direction of the ball.

He moves into position ready to strike the ball in front and to the side.

BAT AND BALL

During the swing, control of the angle of the racket face is vital. Tennis is a 'bat and ball' game. The ball will end up where the strings face at the contact point. Players described as having great 'touch' display great control of the racket face.

He follows through from low to high.

Andy Murray aims for a good contact point.

SPIN

Many players apply spin to the ball. The two most common types are topspin and slice. Topspin makes the ball rotate forward, and slice (or backspin) makes the ball rotate backwards, as it travels. Spin is added because it may be essential on some court surfaces or a vital part of a player's tactics. It may also be used in rallies to confuse an opponent and upset their rhythm.

What does spin do?

Adding spin to a shot affects the following:

- the rotation of the ball
- the ball's flight path through the air
- the bounce of the ball
- the flight of the ball after the bounce.

 Lleyton Hewitt plays a 'lifted' forehand.

 Rafael Nadal plays a topspin groundstroke.

Lifted groundstroke

The ball rotates forward slightly as it flies and bounces in a regular manner.

Topspin groundstroke

The ball rotates forwards as it flies. Its arc is a little higher and it will dip down at the end of its flight. It will generally bounce higher than the lifted groundstroke.

Applying spin

To put (impart) topspin on a shot during a rally, the racket head should start below and finish above the contact point with upward swing. To slice a groundstroke the racket head should start above and finish below the contact point of the ball, making a downward swing.

Effects of spin

The path and angle of the ball's flight before the bounce determines its path and angle after the bounce. Backspin makes the ball skid when hit low, whereas topspin makes the ball bounce higher (or 'kick'). When talking about the serve, 'slice' means sidespin and not backspin.

> Some grips, such as the semi-Western on the forehand (see page 34), help players put spin on the ball.

Sliced groundstroke
The ball rotates backwards. The ball stays in the air longer and the bounce is lower than a lifted groundstroke.

THE SERVE

The action of a serve is essentially a throwing action. The strength of a player's serve is closely related to the strength of their throw.

The serve is the one shot in tennis that you are in total control of, so don't waste this opportunity. Pay close attention to building and grooving your service. Regular serving practice will help build your skills and confidence.

Grip

Some beginners prefer to practise the serve using the Eastern forehand grip. As they become more skilled, they can then adopt the chopper, or continental, grip. The chopper grip is the most effective grip for developing spin and power when serving.

Stance

The starting position is a comfortable sideways position, with your feet shoulder-width apart. Maintaining good balance throughout, throw the ball (known as 'placing the ball') into the air at a comfortable height and slightly towards your target.

With practice, you will be able to work both hands together in rhythm. Try to feel a smooth, coordinated action. All the different parts of your body should be working together not fighting against each other.

The serve is essentially a throwing action.

Contact point

It is a good idea to place the ball just above your full reach (with the racket) so that you hit it when it is almost stationary in the air at full stretch – about twelve o'clock if it were on a clock face, with the ball slightly in front of you.

Action

Your right arm needs to come back into a throwing position, known as the pre-throw or trophy position.

As the ball gets to the top of its rise upwards, accelerate the racket head at the ball in a throwing action. Try to reach up to the ball as you hit it. The higher that you can make contact with the ball the better. Follow through across your body. Look to recover quickly and get ready for your next shot.

Serena Williams demonstrates one of the most powerful serves in the women's game.

Don't rush into the serve, spend time getting your stance right and focus on where you want to aim your serve.

FOREHAND VOLLEY

The forehand volley is a shot played before the ball has bounced on your side of the court. It is most used when a player is approaching or at the net, although, it is sometimes used in the midcourt or even deeper.

Grip

Beginners often use the Eastern forehand grip at first. They are advised, though, to move on to the chopper grip which can make low volleying easier. The chopper grip can be used for either the forehand or the backhand volley, which is particularly useful when there is not enough time to change the grip.

Stance

The stance before the ball arrives is the ready position. On contact, the shoulders should make a half-turn to allow the contact to be made with the ball in front. Stepping towards the ball with the left foot (for right handers) to add strength to the contact can be very effective for beginners learning to volley.

Contact point

As with the backhand volley, the contact should be in front, a comfortable distance to the side and ideally above net height at about shoulder height. In reality, though, this will depend on the speed, height and direction of the incoming ball.

Action

The volley has the simplest and shortest action of all the major strokes. The racket path is from above the height of the ball forwards to below the height of the ball. The action is very short, a little like taking a one handed catch. The angle of the racket face at the point of contact is very important.

PRACTISING VOLLEYS

Practise volleying from a position close to but not right next to the net – about a third of the way back to the service line (the first line you see behind you). Ask another player to hit shots which reach you at around or just below shoulder height.

Serena Williams contacts in front with a short action, using the opponent's power.

Roger Federer steps forward with his left foot as he plays a forehand volley.

BACKHAND VOLLEY

Grip

Some beginners change to an Eastern backhand grip to volley. More advanced players, though, volley with a chopper grip and do not change grip from forehand volley to backhand.

For the two-handed backhand volley the hands are placed next to each other on the grip. This restricts the player's reach, but can help bring greater strength to the shot than with the one-handed grip.

Stance

The stance before the ball comes is the ready position. On contact, the shoulders turn sideways to the ball so that contact is made in front of the player.

Stepping towards the ball with the right foot (for right handers) can help add power to the contact and is also a good learning aid for beginners.

Contact Point

The contact point is similar to the forehand volley. Players using a one-handed backhand volley can make contact further in front of their body. This is because the hitting arm does not have the body in the way as it does with the forehand volley or two-handed backhand volley.

Action

The one-handed backhand volley is similar action to the forehand volley – a short, 'blocking' action. However, the supporting hand stays on the racket until just before the ball is struck.

Tim Henman, a one-handed backhand player, contacts the ball out in front with a short, blocking action.

SMASH

A powerful shot used to hit an overhead ball, the smash requires good timing and concentration. The chopper grip is ideal for smashing, although beginners may use a forehand grip at first.

Stance

As with the serve, this should be sideways to the ball. The position under the ball is similar to that you would take if you were going to 'head' the ball back to the opponent. This should allow you to move forwards into the shot.

Contact point

As with the serve, contact should be at full stretch with the ball slightly in front of you.

> **When hitting a smash try pointing your non-racket hand at the ball. This acts as guide to the ball's flight and helps balance.**

Action

The smash requires fast, balanced footwork to get you beneath the ball. The action is similar to the service. However, the racket is taken back in a shorter movement than the service, almost as if pulling back the string of a bow to shoot an arrow.

 Marat Safin – in balance before he hits the smash.

SHOT VARIATIONS

Lob

The lob is a shot played over an opponent's head when they are at the net. Lobs can be attacking or defensive, to buy time or to attempt a winner. The lob can be played as a backhand or a forehand stroke. The forehand is a little easier to learn and play.

Playing the lob is similar to executing a forehand or backhand drive in grip, stance and contact point. However, the action is different. The racket face is kept more 'open' on contact with the ball and the follow-through is a little higher. You are aiming to use the effect of gravity to drop the ball close to the opponent's baseline.

Andy Murray follows through high as he lifts a lob.

PRACTISING LOBS

During a practice, try to play lobs in between forehand and backhand drives. This will show you how similar the drive and the lob are but how much more control you need for the lob.

> Unless you add topspin, avoid hitting the ball too hard when playing the lob.

Drop shot

The drop shot is a soft shot played on the backhand or forehand side very short into the opponent's court. The ideal aim is to get the ball to bounce twice on the opponent's side of the court before they can reach it. If that doesn't occur, a good drop shot will draw your opponent forward and potentially off balance. This may allow you to attack and win the point with your next shot.

A drop shot is often played with backspin and requires good control of the racket face to take the pace off the ball.

Half volley

A half volley is played immediately after the bounce of the ball. It is often played from the volleying position when a volley is not possible, but also, on occasion, from the baseline.

Imagine throwing a tennis ball at the base of a wall. The angle that the ball bounces up from the wall is similar to the flight path needed for a half volley. Therefore making a 'wall' with the racket face on impact is good basic advice. Control of the racket face is important.

 Roger Federer – a master of the drop shot.

Playing a half volley.

> You can play a drop shot as a volley, which is known as a stop volley.

PLAYING THE GAME

Tennis is a game for life. It's a great, enjoyable way to keep in shape. Unlike other sports, you only have to arrange one other person to play with and you can be flexible how long you play for.

GETTING STARTED

Anyone can play tennis and it doesn't have to cost a lot. To get on court you simply need a pair of trainers, a tennis racket and ball. Joining a club ensures you have access to coaching and great programmes to improve your game, but you can play at your local park for free or on a pay-and-play basis.

LEARNING OR IMPROVING YOUR GAME

You can improve your game in many ways:

- practise with friends
- taking lessons with a coach
- playing in competitions
- joining a tennis club.

Getting coaching will help identify areas of improvement. You can be coached individually or in a group. The cost of coaching varies according to the coach's experience. It can cost as little as £4 per person for a group session and £15–£30 for individual lessons.

Details of coaching, club and school schemes and initiatives in your area can be provided by the LTA Club Development Officer (CDO). These are based at the local LTA county office. To find a club or contact your local CDO for more information, visit www.LTA.org.uk.

Always check your coach has the appropriate qualifications.

TAKING PART IN COMPETITIONS

There are over 2,000 LTA tournaments throughout the country for all ages and abilities. A tennis rating is required to play regularly in competition. Details of the LTA tournaments and how to apply for a tennis rating can be found at www.LTA.org.uk/GetOnCourt.

RAW TENNIS

Raw Tennis is the new face of tennis for young people 10–18 years of age. It's much more than just playing the game, it's about improving skills, learning new activities and having fun getting fit with friends.

What's in Raw Tennis?

There are four areas:

- Freestyle – skills, flicks and tricks
- Energy – getting fit to hit
- Slams – quick-fire team matches
- PBs – tracking and improving skills.

Visit www.rawtennis.net for great downloads, quizzes, news and to find details of a Raw Tennis venue near you.

Raw Tennis – specially designed for young people.

Raw Tennis players practising their freestyle skills.

Being coached as part of a group can be great fun, and it helps to keep the cost down.

ARIEL MINI TENNIS

Ariel Mini Tennis is the modified game of tennis designed for children to have fun whilst they learn the skills of the game. It is suitable for complete beginners or the more experienced young player. It is available at over 800 venues across Britain. These can easily be found by visiting www.arielminitennis.com. The website also includes lots of interactive fun and games for young people.

There are three levels of play – red, orange and green. Age level and racket size will depend on the players' size, strength and ability. Below is a general guide.

	Age	Racket Size
Red	4–8	43–58cm (17–23 in) long
Orange	7–8 and above	58–63.5cm (23–25 in) long
Green	9 and above	63.5–66cm (25–26 in) long

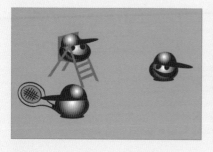

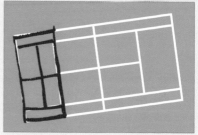

Red

The earliest stage sees children introduced to the basics of the game. They begin to develop core skills like movement and coordination through playing short matches, team competitions and other fun activities. For indoor play an 8cm sponge ball is used. Outside, a Mini Tennis red ball is used. It is larger than a tennis ball and has a gentle, low bounce.

Red level is played in a 12m x 6m area. This can be played across a tennis court or on a badminton court. The net is set 80cm high and the service box measures 4m x 3m.

Orange

During the orange level, children learn new shots and techniques to help them rally longer and better. Competition elements include slightly longer matches, most often played as part of a team with other sports and activities alongside. The ball used at this level is a Mini Tennis orange ball. The size of a normal tennis ball, it is softer and lighter.

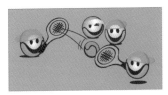

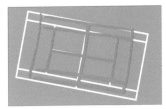

 Orange level is played on a full-width tennis court shortened to 18m in length but with a regular net. Tramlines are used for doubles play.

Green

The final stage of Ariel Mini Tennis prepares children for the full game. Children at this stage will be bigger and more developed and thus able to cover the whole court. They will further improve their technique and tactics, as well as fundamental athletic skills. Matches are longer again, but still mostly in a team environment. The ball used is the same size as a regular tennis ball but slightly softer and lighter.

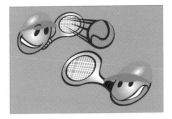

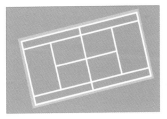

The green level is played on a normal tennis court.

DISABILITY TENNIS AND THE BRITISH TENNIS FOUNDATION

Disability tennis encompasses wheelchair tennis, deaf tennis and tennis for people with learning disabilities. The British Tennis Foundation (BTF), a registered charity that works closely with the LTA, has a Disabilities Tennis Programme that covers all three areas.

There are exciting opportunities from grass roots through to international competition, including the Paralympic Games for wheelchair tennis, the Deaflympics and the World Special Olympics for learning disabilities. For further information, visit www.britishtennisfoundation.org.uk.

GLOSSARY

Ace
A serve which the receiver fails to touch while attempting to return. The server wins the point.

Advantage
The point following deuce. If a player wins the 'advantage' point, he or she wins the game.

Approach shot
A shot played with the aim of getting to the net.

Backhand
A groundstroke hit on the left of the body by right-handed players, and on the right of the body by left-handers.

Baseline
The line at the end of the court.

Big point
A crucial (pivotal) point often deciding which player wins a set or an important game.

Break (of service)
Where the serving player loses the game.

Bye
Free passage into the next round of a tournament.

Centre mark
The small mark halfway across the baseline. When serving, players must remain on the correct side of this mark.

Clay court
A court with a surface made of crushed shale, stone or brick.

Cross court
A stroke played diagonally across the court.

Deuce
A way of saying 40–40.

Double fault
When the server has failed to serve the ball into the service court on both the first and second serve. The server loses the point.

Down the line
A stroke played straight down the side of the court.

Drive
Another way to describe a 'stroke' hit after the bounce.

Drive-volley
A shot hit before the bounce with the technique of a groundstroke.

Drop shot
A shot played to move the opponent forward in the court.

Exhibition matches
Matches arranged as a form of public entertainment. Where players are rewarded with prize money, but no rankings points.

Flat serve
A flat service is hit without spin and follows a low, straight trajectory. Given the high risk of hitting the net, it is generally better suited for first serves.

Forecourt
The front part of the tennis court near the net.

Forehand
A groundstroke played by left-handers to the left of the body, and by right-handers to the right.

Game point
The score when a player only needs one more point to win the game.

Groundstrokes
Any shot, whether forehand or backhand, played after the ball has bounced.

Half volley
A stroke played immediately after the ball has bounced.

Hard court
A tennis court whose surface is made out of cement, concrete or a similar material.

Inside-out forehand
A forehand hit from the backhand side of the court – sometimes known as an 'off forehand'.

Kick serve
A serve with heavy topspin, causing it to change direction when it lands in the service court. Also known as a twist serve.

Let
The call from the net-cord judge when a serve touches the top of the net. Also used to call for the point to be replayed when it is interrupted or in a match without an umpire, used when the players can't agree on a line call.

Love
Zero in tennis language.

Match point
The score when a player only needs one more point to win the match.

Overhead
Describes a stroke played above the head, e.g. a smash.

Overrule
Where an umpire corrects a decision made by one of the judges.

Passing-shot
A stroke played to beat a player at the net.

Tie-break
A game up to seven points for deciding sets where the score has reached 6 games all (see Rules section).

Tramlines
The area at the sides of the doubles court which is not used in singles play.

Umpire
The umpire decides which player has won a point and also keeps the score. In major tournaments the umpire is assisted by line judges.

Unforced error
An error made while under no pressure from the opponent.

Volley
A ball hit before it bounces.

Walkover
When, usually due to an injury, a player proceeds into the next round of a tournament, without having to play the match.

ALL-TIME GREATS

There are a handful of players who can rightfully claim to being among the best players of any generation, but what exactly is it that makes these players among 'The Greatest'. Certainly, each of these legends has won several Grand Slam titles – the four biggest tournaments of the tennis player's calendar that take place in Australia, France, Wimbledon and the USA. Some have won all four in a row – known as winning 'The Grand Slam'.

WOMEN

Margaret Court

Born on July 16, 1942 in Albury, New South Wales, Australia. Court won more Grand Slam titles than any other player. She won 62 Grand Slam titles in singles, doubles and mixed doubles between 1960 and 1975. She won an incredible 24 titles in singles alone, winning the 'Grand Slam'– all four titles in one season – in 1970. Her greatest rival was Billie-Jean King, with their finest match being the Wimbledon final of 1970 which she won 14–12, 11–9 despite having a sprained ankle. Court used her considerable height to her advantage, basing her game on a heavy serve and secure volley, although she was no slouch from the baseline either, as she proved by winning on the clay courts of Paris five times. Probably the least well known of our greats, this may have been because she was seen as shy and softly spoken.

Billie-Jean King

Born on November 22, 1943 in Long Beach, California, USA. During her 20-year career, Billie-Jean won a total of 20 Wimbledon Championships in singles, doubles and mixed doubles. She won her final Wimbledon crown in 1979 in her 19th Wimbledon Championship, partnering fellow all time great Martina Navratilova. In singles, she won a total of 12 Grand Slam titles, including 6 Wimbledon titles. Her most feared opponent was Margaret Court with whom she had some epic matches. Billie-Jean was an aggressive serve-volleyer whose greatest asset was her fiercely competitive nature. Off court she was a pioneer for women's rights, tirelessly promoting the women's tour that was struggling to make its mark at that time.

Chris Evert

Born on Dec 20, 1954 in Fort Lauderdale, Florida, USA. A model of consistency, Chris Evert won at least one Grand Slam title for 13 consecutive years – a record. In total she won 18 Grand Slam singles titles, six less than Margaret Court and tied with Martina Navratilova. During her 20-year career, she had the highest winning percentage of any player in history, and was a Grand Slam semi-finalist a staggering 53 times out of 57 tournaments entered. She had a few rivalries throughout her career, but the greatest of these was her battle with Martina Navratilova, perhaps the best-known rivalry in tennis history. Navratilova eventually came out on top, winning 43 matches against Evert's 37. She was a grinding baseliner who helped popularise the two-handed backhand that is so common in todays game.

Martina Navratilova

Born on Oct 18, 1956 in Prague, Czechoslovakia. Martina Navratilova is often considered to be the greatest of all women Champions, despite winning six fewer Grand Slam singles titles than the Australian Margaret Court. She won a total of 161 singles titles during her glittering career, including a record of 9 Wimbledon singles titles, the last of which she won in 1990 at the grand old age of 34. She also collected two French Open titles, three Australian Open titles and four US Open titles. Her greatest adversary was Chris Evert, whose record of tournament wins she surpassed in Chicago in 1991. Their rivalry was helped by their differing styles – Evert was firmly rooted to the baseline with her pinpoint groundstrokes whereas Navratilova was the game's finest net rusher. The contrast led to several epic matches, mostly in tournament finals.

Steffi Graf

Born on July 14, 1969 in Bruhl, Germany. Steffi Graf burst onto the scene towards the end of the 1980s to snap the dominance that had existed between Navratilova and Evert. In 1988 Graf won an unprecedented Golden Grand Slam. She won all four major titles as well as a gold medal in the Olympics. In total, Steffi won an incredible 22 Grand Slam singles titles, including at least four titles at each tournament, a record.

MEN

Rod Laver

Born on 9 August, 1938 in Queensland, Australia. Considered by many to be possibly the greatest player ever. Laver won a total of 11 Grand Slam titles, although it could have been far higher. Unfortunately, he was unable to compete in any Grand Slam tournaments between 1963 and 1967 because tennis was not yet a professional sport. He won two Grand Slams during his career – the only person to have done so. The first was when the game was still amateur in 1962, and the second was seven years later in 1969. Laver's main rival was Ken Rosewall, another Australian, over whom he held a slight advantage. A left-hander with a huge forearm, Laver had the complete all court game with no apparent weaknesses. He was the first player to consistently attack with a topspin backhand, which was much copied but rarely bettered. Off court, Laver was a quiet unassuming Champion.

Bjorn Borg

Born on 6 June, 1956 in Sodertalje, Sweden. Probably the greatest baseliner of all time, Bjorn Borg confounded the critics by winning five Wimbledon titles in a row, despite having a game more suited to slower courts. He won a total of 11 Grand Slam titles, putting him in third place in the men's game despite having retired at the relatively young age of 26. He won

his first Grand Slam title on the clay courts of the French Open in 1974. In 1976 he won his first Wimbledon title without losing a set and he defended his title four times before losing his crown to John McEnroe in 1981. He eventually won five Wimbledon titles and six French Open titles – but no US Open.

Jimmy Connors

Born on 2 September, 1952 in Illinois, USA. Connors was the greatest on court fighter the game has ever seen. His 'never-say-die' attitude is legendary. Connors won a total of eight Grand Slam titles during his career, equalling other such greats as Andre Agassi and Ivan Lendl. In 1974 he was virtually unbeatable, winning three Grand Slam titles. He perhaps would have won the Grand Slam had he not been prevented from playing in the French Open that year. He had to play second fiddle at Wimbledon to Borg in the late 1970s, but eventually did take a second title there in 1982 with a dramatic victory over John McEnroe. It was against both these players that Connors had his greatest matches. His style was aggressive hitting from the baseline with his double handed backhand in particular a fearsome weapon. Connors was a streetfighter who would regularly whip up the crowd into a frenzy, often helping him win matches from seemingly impossible positions.

John McEnroe

Born on 16 February, 1959 in Wiesbaden, Germany. McEnroe will be remembered as the greatest artist to ever play the game, whose outrageous ability was only equalled by his controversial on court conduct. McEnroe won a total of seven Grand Slam titles – which was probably less than his incredible talent deserved. His first title came at the US Open in 1979 which he held for three years. His first Wimbledon title came in 1981 over Borg, with whom he had been involved in the greatest Wimbledon final of all time in 1980. Indeed, Borg was the greatest of many rivals McEnroe had in his prime – the others being Conners and Lendl. A disappointment came in 1984, in which year he was virtually unbeatable, when he let slip a two set lead against Ivan Lendl in the final of the French Open.

Pete Sampras

Born on 12 August, 1971 in Washington DC, USA. With a record 14 Grand Slam titles to his name, Pete Sampras is currently the all-time no. 1 men's Grand Slam Champion. He won a record seven Wimbledon singles titles, five US Opens and two Australian Opens. For five consecutive years from 1993 until 1998, Pete Sampras was supremely dominant on the men's tour. Indeed he holds the record for the longest time spent at no. 1 – an amazing 286 weeks including that record six consecutive year-end finishes in first position. The only blemish on his record was his inability to win the French Open – and it is this that leads many to claim that he can't be called the greatest ever. His fiercest rival was another legend of the game – Andre Agassi – who did manage to win all four Grand Slams. However, Sampras always had the edge over his more glamorous opponent.

Roger Federer

Born on 8 August, 1981 in Basel, Switzerland. Following so soon after Pete Sampras, Roger Federer is on his way to becoming perhaps the greatest player of all time. He has already won six Grand Slam titles and shows no sign of slowing down. He has won three consecutive Wimbledon titles, joining Sampras and Borg as the only modern players to have done so. In 2004 Federer compiled an astonishing 23–0 record against his fellow top ten players. Federer's game is a beautiful mix of power and skill. He can hit every shot in the book, all while maintaining the balance of a dancer. Charming off court, Federer is renowned for being a genuinely nice guy, at ease with the pressure of greatness.

INDEX